To Be
WELL FED,
WELL SEXED &
WELL RESPECTED

*The Three Things Your Husband
Really Wants From You*

PAMELA A. STOVALL

TO BE WELL FED, WELL SEXED & WELL RESPECTED
©2022 by Pamela A, Stovall

Scriptures marked NKJV are taken from the New King James Version® (NKJV). Copyright © 1982 by Thomas Nelson. Used by permission. All rights reserved

Scripture quotations marked CSB have been taken from the Christian Standard Bible®, Copyright © 2017 by Holman Bible Publishers. Used by permission. Christian Standard Bible® and CSB® are federally registered trademarks of Holman Bible Publishers.

Scripture quotations marked NLT have been taken from the Holy Bible, New Living Translation, copyright ©1996, 2004, 2007, 2013, 2015 by Tyndale House Foundation. Used by permission of Tyndale House Publishers, Inc., Carol Stream, Illinois 60188. All rights reserved.

Scripture quotations marked TPT are from The Passion Translation®. Copyright © 2017, 2018, 2020 by Passion & Fire Ministries, Inc. Used by permission. All rights reserved. ThePassionTranslation.com.

Scripture quotations marked NIV are taken from the Holy Bible, New International Version®. Copyright © 1973 1978 1984 2011 by Biblica, Inc.TM Used by permission. All rights reserved worldwide.

Scripture quotations are from the ESV® Bible (The Holy Bible, English Standard Version®), Copyright © 2001 by Crossway, a publishing ministry of Good News Publishers. Used by permission. All rights reserved.

Contents

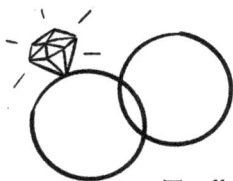

To all those courageous women out there
who have chosen to do marriage God's way!

I call you courageous because it takes a strong person
to push back against the so-called norms
of today's society despite the pressures to conform.
I'm rooting for your success!

Introduction

Over the past several years of being married, and then conducting hundreds of marital coaching sessions with couples, as well as personal coaching with married women, I have come to a few conclusions about men: They are not nearly as complex as women! Actually, they are really pretty comprehensible. And that's not a bad thing!

Women are Complicated; Men Not so Much

Men seem to be pretty simple. I've determined, by living with one and observing many others, that there are three basic things men need to be happy and content: good food, good sex and great respect. Why can't it be that simple for us?

I can't count the number of times I have asked God the question, "Why are women so complicated? As yet, I have not received an answer. I suppose I should just accept it and move on. The problem is, it makes things difficult, sometimes, for our husbands.

In the area of food, for instance, women take the time to determine the quality of the food. Is it healthy, or organic? How much sugar or salt, how much gluten, what kinds of fats are used and on and on and on. We care more about what we put in our mouths than the mere fact of just eating. We want to know how it will affect our waistline; will it help or hurt fine lines and wrinkles on our face; will this particular food enhance my beauty or detract from it. Men just want to eat! When we want to start eating healthily, we feel empowered. Men feel deprived.

Ah, sex! When talking about women being complicated, sex is definitely one of those areas where we are probably the most complex. We're so influenced by our environment, our upbringing, our opinion of ourselves, social media, and the list goes on and on. And, of course, there are those wonderful hormones: Are we PMSing, pre or post-menopausal? Why is this? As my once three-year-old granddaughter use to say, "I noknow."

As far as the respect issue goes, men typically need it more than women. It's what keeps them going and feeling good about themselves. Most women need love and affection. As with any generality, there are always exceptions to the rule; but, typically, most women want to feel secure in our husband's love for us. We delight in hearing those "I love yous" and other words of endearment. Men want to know that we look up to them and think they are the greatest everything. The late Myles Munroe, Bahamian evangelist and ordained minister who founded and led the Bahamas Faith Ministries International, once said this: "A man does not need love!" That sounds shocking on its face, but he went on to explain that men interpret respect as love.

In our efforts to understand our own complexities, we sometimes get frustrated in trying to discover our true purpose in this world aside from childbearing and rearing. I know that I often ask this question also, "God, you put all these gifts in me. What in the world am I supposed to do with them?"

Sometimes we're strong, sometimes we want to dominate, sometimes we just want a shoulder to cry on. Although we may get lost in figuring out who we are, we must recognize that God did not make a mistake when He made us the way He did. Even though we may not understand ourselves, He does. A recent acquaintance of ours, Colonel Richard Toliver, a second generation Tuskegee Airman, has written a book called, *WOMAN, A Godly Creation*. He states this, "God used women to instruct and reveal to me many of the things I needed to know to be a total person."[1] You see, we have so many facets and layers that, although they, perhaps, make us more complicated, God uses those intricacies to help develop and inspire others.

So I guess the conclusion is this: I'm glad I am a complicated woman (most days) who can peel off layers as needed to meet the needs of those I love and influence.

In writing this book, I wanted to have fun with a serious topic: What makes our husbands tick? As with any of the gazillion books on marriage, this one will certainly not solve all your issues, but it will shed some light on some areas that you may not have given much thought about before.

Well Fed, Well Sexed, Well Respected

There are three basic needs that help a man feel fulfilled in his life. They are, to put it succinctly: fun and tasty food, a satisfying sex life, and great respect, especially from their wives or significant others. I suppose I could also throw in doing well in their jobs or career. However, I strongly believe being happy with the former three will facilitate the latter.

To a large number of men, good food is equated with happiness. If all they could eat were fruit, vegetables and grains, their quality of life would be sorely diminished. And if desserts were eliminated from their diets, misery would abound.

In the area of sex, it appears, for the most part, that most of us wives have not realized how important a fulfilling sex life is to our husbands. It's much deeper than just the ejaculatory release they may achieve. I endeavor to help you see that it is imperative that we seek to understand this important need and become more equipped in helping that to be a reality for them and ourselves.

God created men with strong bodies, strong minds but fragile egos. They are able to conquer Herculean tasks, build incredible machines, create exceptional technology. All those things are marvelous and extraordinary; but when it comes to their mates, the least little negative word, used in the wrong tone, will make them feel disrespected, dismissed and minimized. Therefore, we need to learn the art of helping our husbands be their best by holding them in high esteem. From the time my husband and I first married, it was always my endeavor to make sure our home was a place he felt respected. I understood that, as an African-American man, he could be subjected to disrespect and dishonor in society; and I never wanted to be the one who would exacerbate that kind of experience at home. I can't say that I was always successful, but it was certainly a constant goal. This is the topic I spend the most time on because if we get this one right, we'll be miles ahead of the game; and the other two areas might possibly just fall into place.

Getting these three things right in the lives of our men will go a long way in increasing their quality of life. If it's done with a sincere intentions, it will also greatly benefit us, as well.

PART 1
Well Fed

CHAPTER 1

Let the Man Eat!

*"Men become passionately attached
to women who know how to cosset
them with delicate tidbits."*
(Honoré de Balzac – 1799-1859)

We've all heard it, "The key to a man's heart is through his stomach." That may seem like a tired, archaic statement, but the reality is that it is actually true. Men love food, and they especially love comfort food. Here's another one: "Nothing says lovin' like something from the oven."

Many times, in our efforts to be the responsible adult in providing for the health and nutrition of our family, we sometimes start to act like the "momma" and dictate what our husbands should eat. One afternoon, after a meeting, my husband and I were outside chatting with another couple. I suggested to my husband that we go and pick up some tiramisu from the café across the street for dessert later. That prompted a discussion that went something like this:

"If I wanted some dessert like that, my wife would say to me, 'Now, honey, you know you don't need that,'" stated the husband in a snarky, feminine tone.

"That's because I care about your health", she responded.

I stated, "Have you ever noticed how much quicker women are to adapt to a healthy eating program, but men are so much more resistant? I would love to interview a bunch of guys to find out why that is."

"It's because," said the friend, "when we want to get healthy, we want it to be our own decision. Stop trying to emasculate us and trying to be our mommas!"

It was a striking statement but very telling. I'll discuss more about this in the section of "Well Respected."

The truth is, men really do love food, and when we take the time to prepare something really yummy for them, they appreciate it and it makes them more amiable towards us. When I take a departure from our normal, healthy meals and feel compelled to make something like hamburgers and French fries or spaghetti. My husband's response is always, "Oh goodie, fun food!" I see the delight on his face, and it makes me happy in return. Now, my husband is smart enough to know that you can't have a consistent diet of "fun food" and still maintain good health, but a vacation from time to time is certainly called for to maintain his mental health and sense of wellbeing.

CHAPTER 2

How Differently Men and Women View Food?

C o-author Luke Zhu, an assistant business professor at the University of Manitoba in Canada, said a growing body of evidence suggests that diners, consciously or not, associate healthy food with 'femininity' and unhealthy food with 'masculinity.'"[2]

His team decided to investigate the phenomenon after a former White House chef gave an interview about his meal preparation process. Before President Obama's 2009 inauguration, a reporter asked Walter Scheib how he might cater to both Obama and George W. Bush, or "men with different tastes." "I think , he went on to say, "the key word there is 'men'," the chef responded. 'Food at the White House has a tendency to delineate along gender lines as opposed to political lines... Both presidents that I worked with, if we had opened up a BBQ pit or rib joint, they'd be just as happy."[3] On a side note, I recently found out that there is a decadent burger out that has been named after President George W. Bush.

Researchers asked 93 adults which foods they considered manly and ladylike: baked chicken versus fried chicken, diet potato chips versus regular potato chips, baked fish versus fried fish. Respondents consistently labeled the healthier options as "feminine" and the greasier fare as "masculine."[4]

I was watching an episode of "When Calls the Heart", a series on The Hallmark Channel set in the early 1900's. I was particularly fascinated by a scene of when the owner of a successful lumber mill came home to his wife after a very trying day at work. She had an important issue she wanted to discuss with him, so she had the table set with candles. As he entered the door, he caught the aroma of an, obviously, carefully prepared meal. A look of delight washed over his face as he asked her if it was a particular dish. When she confirmed his guess, his joy intensified. What struck me was not the specific food he was about to devour but the pleasure he received from knowing that his wife had prepared one of his favorite meals just for him. Men love food!

It probably doesn't surprise any of us that the root of men's love of steak, burgers, etc. can probably be traced back to the days when our men had to go out to hunt regularly to bring food home to their families, while women were the gatherers of fruit, nuts, berries, etc. However, some of my research has shown that many of these contemporary desires for the less healthy foods have come more from cultural impositions. For instance, I'm sure you've all heard the quote, "Real men don't eat quiche." Actually some "real men" do eat quiche (my husband included) but it had better be accompanied with fries and maybe some bacon, perhaps even a milkshake.

When I was growing up, I was one of those weird kids who actually liked vegetables. No one ever had to coax me to eat the vegetables on my plate. I never noticed, however, whether my brothers liked them or not. That's probably because my strict father would never have allowed any kind of protest to any food placed in front of us. We all were too smart to (or perhaps, too afraid) to step on that land mine. However, I did notice that whenever my brothers could fend for themselves foodwise, they always consumed a lot of junk food. It was typically from outside sources as you'd be hard-pressed to find junk food in our house. My oldest brother's favorite snack was "soda and potato chips", so much so that my mother declared it was the cause of his acne. It was always that combination, not just soda, not just chips but soda and potato chips.

My love of vegetables has not waned one bit, and I remember when Adrian and I first got married, his disdain for any vegetables besides corn and salad surprised me. Oh, he did like green beans but only if they were cooked with bacon and bacon fat. Over the years, of course, he has learned to eat more vegetables and enjoy (more accurately, tolerate) them, but it didn't come easily.

The only veggie I didn't particularly care for as kid was Brussels sprouts. I finally discovered that it was because I didn't know how to properly prepare them. Growing up, we only had the frozen ones that you'd boil. Eew! One Thanksgiving, I decided to try out a recipe for them using fresh ones. After tasting them, I'm almost certain I heard the angels singing, " ♪ AAH-HHH ♪ "! They were absolutely scrumptious, and I couldn't wait to let Adrian try them! Well, suffice it to say that he was not quite as delighted as I. As he took a bite, his face told the whole story. At least I had lots of turkey and dressing and sweet potato pie to keep him happy. It didn't really bother me, though, because it meant more for me. I've tried a few more recipes since then, and he has actually learned to like them. Amazing!

It has been, and always will be, an interesting phenomenon how certain foods bring my palate pure delight where those same foods bring a frown to my husband's face. I've often wondered if it is a genetic thing or a difference in male and female taste buds. I've even notice how one of my granddaughters enjoys veggies, but her brother has to work very hard to swallow his.

According to Amanda McMillan from Health.com, "Considering how closely smell and taste are related, it's not surprising that women also tend to have more sensitive palates than men. In fact, research from Yale University has found that women actually have more taste buds on their tongues. About 35% of women (and only 15% of men) can call themselves "supertasters," which means they identify flavors such as bitter, sweet, and sour more strongly than others. Also of note: Women of childbearing age taste flavors more intensely than younger or older females, and they may also notice increased sensitivity during pregnancy.[5] Perhaps this is why women enjoy certain foods more than men do. It could possibly be that we are able to taste all the subtleties of flavor while men may find those same foods bland and tasteless.

If you are a Food Network *junkie, as I am, you

have probably noticed the shows that are particularly targeted to men. The four that come to mind are Man vs Food; Man, Fire and Food; Burgers, Brews and Ques, and Guy Fieri's "Diners, Drive-ins and Dives". Most of the foods showcased in these programs are not dainty, delicate foods. They are typically robust and full-flavored with very large helpings. Why? Because men love to eat; I mean, really EAT! I recognize that I am generalizing here. I realize that there are many men who are very health conscious. However, from my observations, when men get together for dinner or to hang out, they aren't ordering grilled chicken with a side of broccoli and a salad, along with water for their beverage. More than likely, they will be asking for burgers and fries, barbecued ribs, hot wings, pizza and something carbonated or beer to drink. If it's a steakhouse, it will probably be a large steak with a giant baked potato, and for goodness' sake, don't forget the dinner rolls.

So, How Do I Get My Husband to Eat a More Healthful Diet?

First of all, understand that you can't make your husband do anything he doesn't want to do. Isn't that true for you also? We all want to feel like we're making decisions for ourselves, so be kind and allow your husband to make up his own mind.

Next, get him involved in what he would like to see changed in his diet. Ask him what foods should stay out of the house. If he feels like he has at least a little bit of say so in the matter, he will be more amenable to the modifications.

Further, don't try to make a bunch of changes all at once. Perhaps start with small things like changing the kind of oil with which you choose to cook. Slowly introduce different kinds of vegetables into the diet, prepared in a way that looks appealing.

Finally, remember to reward your husband's efforts with an occasional, perhaps weekly, treat of something home baked or even a great, big sloppy burger. Fun food!

I understand that living in the twenty first century, the dynamics of meal preparation has changed, somewhat. Many are working from home, and many men are now sharing the cooking responsibilities. Since our son's wife landed a principalship at her school, he now has learned to prepare meals from time to time to help out. What's really fun is when he shares recipes he has found with us and his siblings. He gets so excited when he does an especially good job. So, finding ways to make eating an enjoyable experience could, possibly, be easier with both parties contributing. Have a good conversation with each other about it. Perhaps, including mentions of favorite restaurants to visit can create a bit of eager anticipation of a great food night. The bonus of that is now you also have a great date night that might lead to Part Two of this book.

Reflection

WHERE DO YOU GO FROM HERE?

1. How has this section impacted you?

2. How can you apply the things you learned in this section?

3. What can you ask God to help you with?

PART II
Well Sexed

CHAPTER 1

Men and Sex

*"Sex should be used, but in its proper place and time,
according to God's plan. Within that plan
the sexual instinct is a good thing,
a powerful source of life and unity between two beings.
Outside of God's plan, it quickly becomes a means of
division, a source of cruelty, perversion and death."*
(Walter Trobisch)[6]

The subject of sex in marriage can be one the most controversial topics couples tackle. It can cause some of the most joy or pain depending on your perspective. We have been bombarded with sexual images for ages from books, magazines, television, the internet and social media. Unfortunately, most of these portrayals are completely inaccurate, sometimes unrealistic, and require some re-education for both men and women.

According to Dr. Juli Slattery, "One of the biggest differences between you and your husband is the fact that he experiences sex as a legitimate physical need.[7] Just as your body tells you when you're hungry, thirsty, or tired, your husband's body tells him when he needs a sexual release. Your husband's sexual desire is impacted by what's around him but is determined by biological factors, specifically the presence of testosterone in his body."[8]

Typically, once they have experienced a sexual release, men are physically satisfied; but as time goes on, sexual thoughts become more dominant, and they are more easily aroused. The physical need for sexual release intensifies as sperm builds up in the testicles. Their bodies continues to produce and store sperm. Sperm production fluctuates, however, depending on levels of testosterone and how often he experiences of sexual release.[9]

It may help women understand the need for men to release semen by referring to breast-feeding mothers. If you have ever had that experience, you know how uncomfortable it can be when milk builds up in the breast until the baby feeds. If the child is sleeping and unable to nurse, you understand the necessity to get that milk expressed somehow.[10]

Women's sex drive is not so much linked to any physiological need as men, but it is affected by our reproductive cycle and the hypothalamus. The hypothalamus is a region of the forebrain which coordinates both the autonomic nervous system and the activity of the pituitary, controlling body temperature, thirst, hunger, and other systems and involved in sleep and emotional activity as well as sexual activity.[11] That's a lot power for an organ that's about the size of an almond! As women, we are more connected to our emotions when it comes to sexual desire and our hormones play a major role as well. A woman's sexual desire is far more connected to and impacted by emotions than her husband's sex drive is.

While it's true that a man can experience sexual arousal apart from any emotional attachment, sex for him does, indeed, have an emotional and relational impact. When a man is deeply in love with his wife and is unable to achieve a satisfying sex life with her, he can be hurt emotionally because he feels rejected.

Many woman don't really have a clear understanding of how much their husbands want to please them when it comes to the sexual experience. Believe it or not, they are not just in it for that sexual release. That's just the bonus. They want to feel close to us. They want to be able to express their love for us in this intimate way. And God intended it to be that way.

Understanding Your Husband's Sexuality

Most women recognize that their sex drive is not as strong as her husband's. Unfortunately, it's too easy to minimize how much this can affect their relationship. We may feel that, if we're not that interested, he'll just over it. Sadly, that is unlikely the case. He can become filled with resentment and anxiety because he so desires his wife to desire him in return. You may experience times when your husband is short with you or easily annoyed with you or even the children – maybe even downright mean. It could very likely be traced back to the lack of intimacy you are both experiencing. Many men don't necessarily know how to help their wives understand this great need without feeling embarrassed or appearing too needy.

One of the worst things we can do to our husbands is to make having sex with him feel like such a burden. Who wants to participate in anything that feels like drudgery? Your husband wants you to want him. He is attracted to you and wants to feel close to you. Men experience closeness through sex. We want to feel close, too, but where we could be perfectly satisfied with a hug, or just snuggling on the sofa with a blankie and a bowl of popcorn, (our husbands may enjoy that as well), they, most likely, are becoming aroused and would like more.

It may be true, however, that the men have not fully understood all the things that go on long before the sex act that must be taken into consideration in order to put his wife "in the mood": how has he treated her, how does she feel about herself, how is her physical health? Even this, though, is no excuse to refuse your husband's advances. Understand that he is reaching out to you and allowing himself to become very vulnerable to rejection.

When men get married, they have an expectation that now they will be able to have sex with their wife any time they desire. It's not long after the honeymoon that they get a reality check. Men's and women's libido don't function in the same way and at the same time. As already mentioned, typically, men have a stronger drive than women. Consequently, they think about it a lot more than woman do; and because they think about it more, they want to participate in it more.

I once knew a young man who was soon to be married. Right up until the wedding, he was so excited. You see, he was 29 years old and had remained a virgin in anticipation of a God-ordained relationship. It was said that on the day after his wedding night, his face beamed with joy. I felt great happiness for him but also a bit of sadness as I knew that there was going to come a time in the relationship that he and his bride would not be on the same sexual page. In other words, he waited all these years so that he could be intimate with her forever, whenever he wanted; but she won't necessarily have that same goal unless she had truly been taught to understand the sexual needs of her husband and the gift God intended sex to be.

Women can be very dismissive when it comes to their husbands and sex. Women just don't think about sex as much as men do. It's very easy for us to be busy with life: chasing after children, carting them back and forth to soccer practices and games or dance recitals, etc., working a full-time job then coming home to household duties and the like. You get the picture. By the end of the day, we are exhausted, and all we want to do is go to bed and actually sleep – not fool around – SLEEP! Men, on the other hand can work an exhausting job, be tired as a dog and still have sex on their minds. Their desire for sex can easily trump their desire for sleep.

When we recognize the stronger need of sex in our husband's life and choose to ignore it, we are sending them the message, "That's your own personal problem, and I don't care." There are two responses we could possibly have in this situation, and both are damaging to the relationship. One is that we completely discount their desires and needs, and the other is that we make ourselves available to them, but our hearts are not the least bit in it. What we are communicating to our husbands is that we don't really care about them. They, consequently, feel unloved, undesirable, unattractive and less than a full man. Think about how you feel when you husband hasn't paid much attention to you or told you that he loves you in a while. What thoughts go through your mind? You probably feel unloved, undesirable and unattractive.

Reflection

WHERE DO YOU GO FROM HERE?

1. How has this section impacted you?

2. How can you apply the things you learned in this section?

3. What can you ask God to help you with?

CHAPTER 2

You Have All the Power

We women have to be so careful not to use sex as a reward or withhold it as punishment. It can become, if not put in its godly place, a weapon of dual destruction. I say dual because it hurts you both. I spoke with a young woman who told me how she made an attempt at initiating sex with her husband after realizing that she had been neglectful in that area. She felt hurt because he apparently rejected her advances. I happened to share the information with my husband. His response was passionate, "Why can't women understand that they have all the power! When men keep getting rejected that way, they can shut down those feelings and completely back off in order not to experience the hurt feelings of rejection and denial. " I thought a lot about what he said and realized that he was right, especially about the power. Men desire the intimacy and closeness of the sexual experience with their wives, but can only have it with a willing partner. Otherwise, they are left to feel empty and alone. If he is a faithful man, he is not going to go looking for a release through infidelity; so he suffers either in silence or in anger.

The only way a man has power over a women in the area of sex is through rape. Rape is a heinous crime, and no one should ever experience it. It should be noted that, according to experts, rape is never really about sex at all; it's about control. *"Rape and sexual assault are not sexually motivated acts. Rather, they stem from aggression, rage, and the determination to exercise power over someone else, according to a widely cited 1992 report.*[12]

"You Might Just Get Lucky Tonight."

How many women have used that phrase with their husbands? This was my premise of how that statement would be interpreted: It's basically saying that if her husband acts a certain way, or says the right things or bows to her wishes, then she will reward him with sex. In my opinion, this was not only insulting, but it made the whole idea of a holy, consecrated union menial and pedestrian. In other words, I thought, when I tell my husband he might just get lucky tonight, it means I am giving him something that would be considered a reward for good behavior. That is not the purpose of sex.

God intended it to be a mutually satisfying experience to celebrate our love for each other. It is also not simply for procreation. I was pretty sure that I was correct in my assessment of the statement, but read on.

I was very curious how men actually do respond to that statement, internally, so I conducted a blind survey. Understand that this was by no means an actual scientific sampling, but it did reveal some interesting information.

I must confess that only one gentleman actually confirmed my theory. He wrote, "I must be on my best behavior because if I am, I'll be rewarded." All the rest of the responses revealed how important and enjoyable sex was to men. Here are a few more:

"I would be very excited and look forward to the evening."

"I'd feel like a very happy man."

"Dang! Okay, any plans I need to change, I will."

"Sorry boys. Something came up and I will not make it tonight."

These next few I'll share, in my opinion, give the most insight to how men think when it comes to having sex with their marriage partner:

"It makes me feel valued, appreciated and happy knowing that my wife wants me."

"Once I thought about it for longer than a moment,

what I felt was that she meant we would have a few minutes to relax and the kids would actually be easy and there would be no 'serious' decisions that needed to be made. We would be able to enjoy each other's company. I don't need luck for sex; I get plenty of that. I need the stars to align to spend quality time with my best friend."

"Being married for ten years, this type of quality time is hard to accommodate with two small kids. However, this statement is no guarantee it will happen as the key word is 'might', LOL! It makes me feel good knowing my wife is still playful and hints at something that makes me want her that much more."

"It makes me feel loved, wanted and connected. I know without hesitation or question how I feel about my wife; all the reasons I like to look at her, touch, feel and study her. To be reminded that she wants and thinks of these things, for and with me too, is reassuring in making me feel like she's all I ever wanted. So, yes. It makes me feel excited and expectant for what's to come. For me, that is great, but I can have a similar feeling simply from my thoughts towards her throughout the day. Her invitation is icing on the cake."

After those last three responses, I understood that men simply want to have a quality, sexual relationship with the wife they cherish. So, obviously, we as wives must learn how to navigate our schedules to include quality time with our husbands that end with lovemaking.

As you can see, I was mistaken in my understanding of the statement, "You might just get lucky tonight!" I stand corrected!

Reflection

WHERE DO YOU GO FROM HERE?

1. How has this section impacted you?

2. How can you apply the things you learned in this section?

3. What can you ask God to help you with?

CHAPTER 3

The Sex Talk

For those of you have grown or teenaged children, I'm sure you remember the anticipation of having to have "the sex talk" with them. The idea of doing it was not the most comfortable feeling, especially, trying to figure out the right timing and the words. You knew it was a necessary and responsible part of parenting, but the thought of it was not thrilling.

Well, the idea of having "the sex talk" with your spouse can be just as intimidating. However, it must be done in order to bring resolution to some of the difficulties that couples have in this area.

At this point, I would be remiss in not addressing the fact that I know some of you reading this book may have experienced serious trauma in your life in regards to sex, and that it may be adversely affecting your ability to fully give yourself to your husband, sexually. If you have been sexually abused as a child or even as an adult through rape, molestation, etc., I implore you! Please do not neglect getting counseling or therapy to heal from it. It's also important that you make your husband aware of the trauma. He needs to know about it so he can help with the healing process. I would even recommend allowing him to attend the counseling with you, at some point, so he has a better understanding of why you may be having intimacy issues.

Since we now have a better idea of how important sex is to our husbands, how do we bridge the gap between our needs and desires and that of our husbands? The only way for it to happen is to Communicate with a capital C. If we are determined to make our husbands feel more satisfied in this area, it is vital that we help them understand how *we* "work". We must, somehow, convey to them what it takes to get (or keep) us "in the mood"; and if not in the mood, at least happily willing and available. There has to be a compromise developed to make sure that all parties are satisfied so that we women don't feel like mere sex objects. One word of caution, though. If you start the conversation with, "We need to talk!", be prepared for some resistance and defensiveness. Men get very uncomfortable with those words, so the gentle approach is best.

Our hormones play such a huge role in our sex life. It has to drive men crazy! For us, the mood has to be right, we want to feel well physically, there has to be an environment created for it. In other words, if we have had a particularly hectic day with no time to process or relax, the idea of sex is the furthest thing from our minds. And because our minds are constantly busy with multi-tasking, sex does not dominate our thoughts as it does with men. Even when we feel fully ready for sexual activity, what turned us on a few days ago may be different now. There is no magic formula that men can follow to be assured of success. Our bodies and feelings change with our hormones.

We, women, are in such need of allowing God to help us understand ourselves better. I guess we can't really expect our poor husbands to fully "get" us when we don't fully "get" ourselves, but the necessity to try is paramount.

There have, of course, been many studies about the differences between men and women sexually. That's why the "sex talk" is so important to help your man understand you better so that you can experience the full joy of the experience of intimacy with him. In their book, The Act of Marriage, Tim and Beverly LaHaye explain a number of factors that enhance the sexual experience for women. They specifically describe how woman first need the assurance of her husband's love by way of companionship, compassion and empathy, romance, affection and passion.[13] Let your husband know that you want him to tenderly tell you how he desires you and that he finds you fascinating. That's a word my husband tells me when I find him watching me as I busy myself with things around the house or cook dinner. That makes me feel very special.

Why Should I Care?

Many times when women get married, whether virgins or not, they assume that their new husbands are fairly expert in lovemaking and depend on them to make it a pleasurable experience . Unfortunately, that's not always true; and as a result, the new bride winds up with a disappointing encounter that creates a bad memory and now sex becomes dreadful instead of something delightful in which to look forward.

Some women go into marriage with great expectation for a wonderful experience, while others have already been brainwashed into thinking that it is something they simply tolerate or endure for their husbands' sake. The latter could not be further from the truth.

Sex has become the most discussed but least understood aspect of human life. I think it's fair to say that we, at the end of the twentieth century, are living in the

Sexual Dark Ages. We hear more about sex than our parents or grandparents ever heard, but we understand much less.[14] Well into the twenty first century, we still understand very little.

Why should you care? Simply put, God did not create sex for the man only, neither did He fashion it just for procreation. It was intended to be an intensely pleasurable experience for both the man and woman.

Some notable experts had this to say about the benefits of being actively involved, sexually with your mate:

There are both physical and psychological benefits to having sex on a regular basis. It has cardiovascular benefits: according to a 2010 study, "Men with active sex lives are less likely to develop heart disease; and it has benefits for the prostate", says Dr. Peter Kanaris, a clinical psychologist and sex therapist based in Smithtown, New York.[15] "Not only does sexual intimacy foster a feeling of well-being, it can also have positive effects on the immune system"[16]

"Sex releases endorphins and creates a feeling of closeness between you and your husband", says Mary Andres, a University of Southern California professor in marriage and family therapy.[17]

"Sexual intimacy is more than the bringing together of sexual organs, more than the reciprocal sensual arousal of both partners, more than mutual fulfillment in orgasm. It is the experience of sharing and self-abandon in the merging of two persons, expressed by the biblical phrase 'to become one flesh'."[18] (Howard J and Charlotte H. Clinebell)

Reflection

WHERE DO YOU GO FROM HERE?

1. How has this section impacted you?

2. How can you apply the things you learned in this section?

3. What can you ask God to help you with?

CHAPTER 4

If You Reject His
MALENESS,
You Are Rejecting Him

Your husband's sex organ is part of his body just like his foot, hand or elbow are, so if you reject that part of him, you are, in essence, rejecting *him*. There are many women who express devoted love for their husbands but have no interest in sex. Obviously, there a multitude of reasons why this is true. The problem is that it is, *indeed*, a problem – a very big problem! It's a problem because the "maleness" of a man is part of who he is. And when we commit to a marital relationship, we must commit to all of it. It's like saying you want a pizza, but you only want the crust. Umm, that's not a pizza. This is not to put you on a guilt trip if that describes you. It is simply to cause you to see why this is not something that should be left unaddressed.

It's very important that you be the initiator, at times. This sends a strong message to your husband that you find him desirable. It also tells him that you love him. I know that sometimes it appears that men are perfectly happy with a quick "wham, bam thank you ma'am". However, a married, committed husband wants more than that. He wants to feel wanted and not that you have merely placed him on a list of all the other things you *have* to get done.

Just because sex is so important to your husband, that does not make him a pervert. He is simply functioning the way God created him. And because it is so important to him, it should also be important to you. God wants married people to enjoy the sexual experience to its fullest. How you do it and what you do are *your* business if it's mutually agreed upon. Lester Sumrall stated this in his book, *60 Things God Said About Sex*, "No kind of sexual pleasure is 'off limits' to a husband and wife, so long as it honors God. Some people think that only one particular technique of lovemaking is 'holy', and all others are sinful; but you won't find that teaching in Scripture."[19] I fully agree. This is another reason why the "sex talk" is so important.

Learning to appreciate your husband's differences from you is critical to learning how to enjoy each other in all areas of your life, not just sexually. Don't take the gift God has given you for granted or treat it with disdain and dread. Embrace it! Ask Holy Spirit to help you in any area you feel you come up short. I wonder, sometimes, if women are actually reluctant to ask God to help them in the area of sex because they feel embarrassed. Please remember that God is interested in every area of our lives. He wants us to achieve victory in everything we're concerned about, and sex is not excluded from EVERYTHING!

Show off Your Beautiful Body!

I can already hear the wheels of protest rolling around in your minds. "Are you crazy?! I've gained 50 pounds since we got married. Nobody wants to see that." "You must be kidding! My stretch marks have stretch marks!" "Not on your life. I don't look anything like the women I see on T.V. I'm sure my husband is grateful that I hide my body." I once heard a comedienne joke about that this way, " When we were first married, I'd walk around naked much to my husband's delight. After a number of years of having babies, gaining weight and the like, whenever I walked around nude, he'd ask, 'Aren't you cold?'" That's how a lot of us think, but we are so wrong.

We now live in the age of embracing our bodies no matter what they look like. That's one of the reasons I love Dove. products. They celebrate the real beauty of women. In fact their website says this, "Beauty is not defined by shape, size or color – it's feeling like the best version of yourself. Authentic. Unique. Real."

Here's the deal: Men are visually stimulated; and when you hide from your husband, where else is he going to get that stimulation if he can't look at you. The truth of the matter is that men love looking at women's bodies, so if your husband can't see yours, he'll look elsewhere. Here's another truth: when your husband is in love with you, he's really not that concerned with what your body looks like, especially if you are actively intimate with him. I know that's hard to believe, but it really is true.

Another important component in showing off your beauty is confidence. This may be one of those areas where you have to fake it 'til you make it. When a woman displays confidence in her ability to keep her husband interested in her sexually, that's a total turn-on to him. I had a friend many years ago who used to boldly declare, "I defy any woman to take my place!" Now that was probably confidence on steroids, but she meant it because she really believed it. I think her husband believed it, too. Obviously, not all of us can expect to attain that level of self-assurance, but we can certainly ask God to help us get better at it.

Reflection

WHERE DO YOU GO FROM HERE?

1. How has this section impacted you?

2. How can you apply the things you learned in this section?

3. What can you ask God to help you with?

PART III

Well Respected

CHAPTER 1

Fiddler on the Roof

One of my family's favorite movies (including our grandchildren, believe it or not) is "Fiddler on the Roof", a musical comedy adapted from the play and based on the short story: "Tevye and His Daughters by Sholom Aleichem. I have a particularly favorite scene where Tevye and his wife, Golde have an exchange regarding their love for each other. Tevye and Golde had an arranged marriage, but their daughters want to get married for love which was considered a strange idea during those times. With it heavy on Tevye's mind, he decides to ask Golde if she loved him. Her first response in a song was:

> "For twenty-five year I've washed your clothes
> Cooked your meals, cleaned your house
> Given you children, milked the cow
> After twenty-five years, why ask about love
> right now?"

Tevye reminds her how the first time they met was on their wedding day, but his parents said they'd learn to love each other; so he asks her again, "Do you love me?" Now, speaking to the audience, Golde sings:

"For twenty-five years I've lived with him

Fought with him, starved with him

Twenty-five years my bed is his

If that's not love, what is?"

Tevye concludes, "Then you love me?"

Golde confesses, "I suppose I do" , and Tevye finally responds, "And I suppose I love you, too."

They then say together:

"It doesn't change a thing

But even so

After twenty-five years

It's nice to know."[20]

Tevye and Golde grew in love with each other as they played their respective roles of providing security and respect.

During Biblical times, most marriages were arranged, and there are many cultures even today where that is still the case. There are several statistics out there that conclude that fewer arranged marriages tend to end in divorce versus "love-based" marriages. Of course, it must be considered that many of these cultures have a strong stigma attached to the idea of divorce. It must also be considered that there are those cultures where wives may be killed instead of divorced; so although the statistics are very low compared to American culture, those factors must be taken into account. However, even with that information, arranged marriages still have a considerably low rate compared to the United States. Aside from the two stated possible reasons, now the question is why?

The flaw in a love-based marriage is that as soon as the "love" feelings fade, the marriage deteriorates When I speak of a love-based marriage, I'm talking about love that is based on feelings. In other words, the attitude of "you don't make me feel good anymore" creeps in and it now it is all about you and your feelings and your desires. I believe the reason an arranged marriage works is because both parties enter in with an understanding that feelings do not necessarily play a role in how the marriage succeeds. Consequently, they go into it with the understanding that there are two basic needs that must be met in order to achieve success. The husband recognizes that his wife has a need to feel secure and that she will be taken care of. The wife understands that respect is the essential part needed for her husband. As those two needs are fulfilled, and as the marriage matures, the affection for each other grows. But it started with respect and security as with the case of Tevye and Golde.

CHAPTER 2

That Respect Thing

I f you've ever wanted the key to your husband's heart, it's necessary to understand why honor (another word for respect) is so important to him. The fact is, that is how God created him. God created us in His image, and one of the ways you demonstrate your love to Him is through praise. Your husband is the same. Look at Ephesians 5:33: *Nevertheless let every one of you in particular so love his wife as himself; and the wife see that she reverence her husband* (KJV). To shed even more light, let's look at it in the Amplified Bible: *33 However, each man among you [without exception] is to love his wife as his very own self [with behavior worthy of respect and esteem, always seeking the best for her with an attitude of lovingkindness], and the wife [must see to it] that she respects and delights in her husband [that she notices him and prefers him and treats him with loving concern, treasuring him, honoring him, and holding him dear]*

(AMPC). That's about as clear as a bell! Men respond to praise and admiration. It prompts them to do even more to continue to receive that praise. Of course, women respond to it as well, but not nearly the same way men do.

Some of you are still waiting for greatness to come out of your husbands. Guess what? You are the vehicle through which it will be brought out. It's almost as though hearing those words of praise and encouragement are like a super-hero cape has been thrown on him; and now he can vanquish all the evil in the world.

"Behind every great man is an admiring wife." Your husband needs you to be proud of him. He needs to know that you think the world of him; that if nobody else thinks well of him, his wife does. Your husband needs to feel that when he walks across that threshold into his home, he is the most important person on the face of the earth to you. Men need love, but for them love is demonstrated through respect.

The irony of this is that women tend to be far more critical of their husbands than complimentary. They have been somehow convinced that criticism is what will motivate change. Just the opposite is true. Criticism causes your husband to be defensive and rebellious. It will give him reasons to find other things to do than spend time with you. Who wants to be around someone who constantly makes them feel bad about themselves? Admiration, on the other hand, causes him to be energized; it motivates him to do better. God did not bring us to Himself through devaluation. Instead,…*therefore with lovingkindness have I drawn thee* (Jeremiah. 31:3, KJV). My goal is to encourage you to be like Christ in your relationship with your husband.

Simply put, men thrive on admiration. Therefore, ladies, if you want to see your husband succeed; if you want to see your marriage flourish; if you want to have your husband do the little (and big) things you desire from him, lavish him with honor, praise, and admiration. I promise, you will be astonished at the results! Could this take on the nefarious act of manipulation? Absolutely! However, if your heart is pure before God, that will not be your motivation. Instead, you will see it as your responsibility to God to love your husband in the manner God would have you do so.

I know some of you may be saying to yourselves that your husband has no redeemable qualities worth praising. Ask God to bring to your remembrance when you first met him and the things that drew you to him. They're not all gone. There is still something left for you to admire about your husband. Even if it is simply that you appreciate how he goes out every day to work and supports the family. Verbalize it, and make him feel like he can go out and conquer the world because every man wants to feel that way. Just start by noticing the small things and work up to the bigger ones, but make a huge deal of even the small ones. The more you praise, the more he'll give you reason to do so.

He May Not be Perfect, But...

Here's a little something worth tucking under your hat as you consider ways to honor and admire your husband. Men are most attracted to people who make them feel good about themselves. Many times when a man becomes unfaithful to his wife, it's not because he's found someone prettier or someone with a more shapely body than his wife. It's usually because there is another woman who thinks the world of him, and doesn't hesitate to let him know it. *She* finds no fault with him. *She* thinks he is perfect. *She* believes he walks on water. *She* is the one he wants to spend time with if all he gets when he's home is nagging and criticism. Proverbs 7:21-23 gives an important warning: *So she seduced him with her pretty speech and enticed him with her flattery. He followed her at once, like an ox going to the slaughter. He was like a stag caught in a trap, awaiting the arrow that would pierce its heart. He was like a bird flying into a snare, little knowing it would cost him his life* (NLT). Meditate on that for a while.

On the other hand, being a champion of your husband and profusely bestowing praise on him, almost makes him immune to other women's admiration. (I said almost – no hundred percent guarantee here). *You* need to be his most enthusiastic fan.

Just so we are clear, although your mistreatment of your husband may contribute to his desire to look elsewhere for female admiration and support, in no way does it excuse adultery or even an emotional affair. Your husband will always be accountable to God for His behavior. You are never fully to blame, but you must be willing to own the part you may have played.

Reflection

WHERE DO YOU GO FROM HERE?

1. How has this section impacted you?

2. How can you apply the things you learned in this section?

3. What can you ask God to help you with?

CHAPTER 3

The Healing Tongue of a Wise Woman

H ow we speak to our husbands have a great impact on them. Therefore, when it comes to minding our words, we can look, again, to Proverbs for wisdom: *When she speaks, her words are wise, and she gives instructions **with kindness*** (Pro. 31:26, NLT). *Her husband can trust her, and she will greatly enrich his life. She brings him good, not harm, all the days of her life* (Pro 31:11-12, NLT).

Did you know that you have the power to create an atmosphere of success in your homes by the words you speak? Like it or not, I truly believe we are the ones who set the tone of the home. I know you've all heard the saying, "If Mama ain't happy, ain't nobody happy!"

God created the world by His words and because we have been created in His image, our words are also creative. Words are not empty—they have **POWER!!** They can take on a life of their own to shape your life and the life of your home.

Let's take a look at Pro. 18:21: *Death and life are in the power of the tongue: and those who love it will eat its fruit. (NKJV)* One thing that is commonly said about women is that we love to talk. Obviously, that is a generalization because not *all* women love to talk; but it is typically true. However, here is a cautionary proverb to consider: *When there are many words, sin is unavoidable, but the one who controls his lips is prudent.* (Proverbs 10:19, CSB) That, obviously, applies to men and woman; so one could easily conclude that those who don't talk very much probably stay out of trouble more. In fact, to further sharpen the point, Proverbs 21:23 says it this way: *The one who guards his mouth and tongue keeps himself out of trouble* (CSB).

My goal is to show you how we can use that wonderful organ God gave us to bring healing and comfort and life into our environment by using our words carefully and wisely. I want to lay a foundation, first, of how our words can be damaging, and then show how to change the course.

Proverbs 31:26 tells us this, *She opens her mouth with wisdom: and in her tongue is the law of kindness.(NKJV)* The Passion Translation says it this way, *Her teachings are filled with wisdom and kindness as loving instruction pours from her lips.*

Dangers of the Undisciplined Tongue

First *of all, it defiles you.*

Matthew 15:10-11 – *Summoning the crowd, he told them, "Listen and understand: It's not what goes into the mouth that defiles a person, but what comes out of the mouth—this defiles a person. (*CSB)

James 3: *6 And the tongue is a fire. The tongue, a world of unrighteousness, is placed[a] among our members. It stains the whole body, sets the course of life on fire, and is itself set on fire by hell.* (CSB)

These Scriptures are so direct that they're almost jarring, but don't reject them out of hand. Let's take ownership of our actions and receive the knowledge of how the Lord is trying to teach us the way to live victoriously.

Second, *you are put in the same category as the wicked.*

Ps. 64:2-3 – *Hide me from the scheming of wicked people, from the mob of evildoers, who sharpen their tongues like swords and aim bitter words like arrows.* (CSB)

Third, *you become a demolition expert.*

Pro. 14:1 – *Every wise woman builds her house, but a foolish one tears it down with her own hands.* (CSB)

Your harsh, life-stealing words can destroy. You might as well get out the sledge hammer and other tools and start tearing down the house with your very own hands. Harsh words cut, and if heard often enough, will begin to diminish the self-esteem of the hearer. Low self-esteem causes one's dreams to be extinguished because you feel unworthy of even dreaming. Trust and communication are also wrecked because the destruction causes your husband to put up his own new walls. He can't trust you with what's in his heart because you can so easily use his words as a weapon against him later.

How You are Perceived in Your Home Without a Disciplined Tongue!

First, *as someone undesirable to be around.*

Pro. 21:9 *It is better to live in a corner of the housetop than in a house shared with a quarrelsome wife* (someone who loves to pick fights). (ESV) [my parentheses]

Ask yourself this question: If my husband seems to rather spend time with other people than with me, what might be the reason? This is not an accusation, but I do want you to analyze your own actions and words.

Second, *as someone who is foolish and ignorant.*

Pro. 9:13 – *The foolish woman is restless and noisy; She is naive and easily misled and thoughtless, and knows nothing at all [of eternal value]* (AMP).

Third, *as someone who is a nag!*

Pro. 27:15-16 - *A quarrelsome wife is like the dripping of a leaky roof in a rainstorm; (she doesn't even know that her harshness is a turn-off)* [my parenthesis] (NKJV)

I remember when one of the homes my family lived in had roof damage. The way we found out was during a rain storm, and our ceiling sprang a leak. There was nothing to do to remedy the situation at the time except to place a bucket under the leak to catch the rain. It was the most annoying sound listening to that constant dripping in the bucket. We were all so thankful when the leak was finally repaired.

To the women who have unsaved husbands or husbands who are not walking in the word: Your pleading and cajoling is not what will bring him to Christ. First Peter 3:1-2 clearly states, In the same way, wives, submit yourselves to your own husbands so that, even if some disobey the word, they may be won over without a word by the way their wives live when they observe your pure, reverent lives (CSB).

In the beginning of the section, Well Fed, I shared the response to a question directed to the gentleman regarding why men are so resistant to wives encouraging their husbands to eat healthily. He basically said that they wanted it to be their own decision maker and that we (wives) shouldn't emasculate them. When we nag our husbands or try to make decisions for them, we are basically treating them like a children. God has given us the control of our children but not of our husbands. Our husbands are adults with minds of their own. That doesn't mean you cannot have input regarding their decisions, but, ultimately, they are responsible for themselves. We should never try to take matters into our own hands regarding their mental, physical, and social health without their consent. Afterall, they didn't marry us to be their mothers. They married us to be their partners.

Reflection

WHERE DO YOU GO FROM HERE?

1. How has this section impacted you?

2. How can you apply the things you learned in this section?

3. What can you ask God to help you with?

CHAPTER 4

How to Use Your Tongue to Give Life and Healing

O ne of the main ways to do give life and healing in our home is to retrain our mouths! If
we are going to change our ways, we must
first change our minds. We need to thoroughly convinced that badgering our husbands to change or do
something we want only makes him stubbornly dig his
heels in and refuse to do your bidding. Or he will relent
and feel totally impotent, filled with resentment and
dread. He will find reasons to not come home or to
escape to a man cave or garage.

We need to see our husbands through God's eyes.
That takes discipline. So, how does God see them? Our
husbands have been created in His image. God placed
in them characteristics like Himself. He sees the huge
potential they possess, and He sees them as someone

who needs His love and mercy. They are God's image bearers. When we see them that way, we'll change how we speak to them. And we mustn't forget the Golden Rule. We treat our husbands the way we want to be treated.

Speaking Blessings Instead of Curses

James tells us in verse 3:10, *"Blessing and cursing come out the same mouth. My brothers and sisters, these things should not be this way."* (CSB). In other words, we can choose which one we will participate in. When you call your spouse or child stupid, you are cursing them. When you tell them they will never amount to anything, you are cursing them.

"The Lord God has given me the tongue of the learned that I should know how to speak a word in season to him who is weary" (Isaiah 50:4 NKJV). We have the power to speak curses or blessings, but we have to make the choice. God teaches us how to speak with wisdom and to speak at the appropriate time. Sometimes, our words need to be few. This is a place where our tongues can be the most healing of all – saying nothing! Again, When there are many words, sin is unavoidable, but the one who controls his lips is prudent ((Pro. 10:19 CSB). Another example of this is Ps. 141:3, Set a guard, O Lord, over my mouth; Keep watch over the door of my lips [to keep me from speaking thoughtlessly] (AMP).

There were times, during my childhood, that my parents would argue ferociously, and the language they used was disgraceful. My father would say something harsh to my mother, and she would be even harsher in her retort. It always escalated to the point they would actually come to blows. My siblings and I watched in horror as our parents physically fought each other. Whenever an argument started, from a distance, we would say amongst ourselves, "Mommy, just be quiet! If you would just not respond, it would be over with!" But she just couldn't resist trying to get in the last hurtful word. In Ephesians 4:29, we find,

Let no corrupt communication proceed out of your mouth, but that which is good to the use of edifying, that it may minister grace unto the hearers (KJV). Another word for grace here is encouragement.

Ephesians 5 commands a woman to respect her husband , and it doesn't qualify as to whether they've earned it or not. When my husband and I coach couples, we hear from the wives, over and over again, that their husbands have done something to cause them to lose respect for them; so the typical solution in these wives way of thinking is so to deny him that respect. The respect that is commanded in Scripture is not predicated on deservedness. It's based on our obedience. So, then, how can you develop a respectful attitude when you're feeling disillusioned, hurt or angry. First of all, know that you have an enemy who is always going to be whispering in your ear and rehearsing to you the failures of your husband. You have a choice here: Either listen to and agree with the devil or decide to renew your mind with the Word of God. Regardless of your background or experiences, our compliance to God's Word is paramount! And remember, you are not in this alone. Here is where allowing Holy Spirit's wisdom, comfort and urging are so important. He's there to empower us to be submitted to God's Word.

Feeding your mind and heart with the Word is key to getting over hurts. Developing an arsenal of scriptures you can use to remind you of the decision you will need to make in order to operate as a Kingdom wife. First of all, forgiveness must be done. Forgiveness is not a feeling; it's a decision, but let's be real. Just because you make the decision to forgive, Satan will give you every opportunity to forget all about that decision. He will taunt you with memories of the infraction. He will try to convince you that your husband can't possibly deserve to be forgiven and therefore, can't possibly deserve your respect. However, you can combat those thoughts with the powerful scripture found in

2 Corinthians 10:3-5, (CSB) *For although we live in the flesh, we do not wage war according to the flesh, since the weapons of our warfare are not of the flesh, but are powerful through God for the demolition of strongholds. We demolish arguments and every proud thing that is raised up against the knowledge of God, and we take every thought captive to obey Christ.* In other words, here you make a flat-footed declaration not to accept and or give credence to the thoughts Satan places in your minds. The imagery is see is almost like a cartoon bubble over my head that I reach up and take down, and I replace it with a scripture. Scripture memorization is so important! It's our greatest weapon against the wiles of our Enemy.

"How do I get my husband to talk to me?"

Many women, over the years, have ask me that question. The first thing I tell them is nagging won't do it. The next thing I tell them is that trust has to be developed between the two of you. What do I mean by that? He needs to know that he can trust you with what's on his heart without worrying whether you will go off on him, whether you will shame him, or – and this is the worst – that you will share it with your friends and/or family. Dr. David Clarke has written an insightful book called, Men are Clams, Women are

Crowbars.[21] It's a wonderful and humorous look into the differences between men and women and how they communicate. Many times, in our efforts to get our husbands to talk to us, we go about it the wrong way. We push and prod to no avail, and we don't always do it in sweet way. The more we push, the more they resist. Until your husband knows that he can trust you with the things on his mind and heart, he will keep them to himself. Your harsh attempts or cutting tongue will only thrust him further away.

It's such a mystery to me, how women can speak so sweetly and kindly to people outside their homes and yet let venom spew out of their mouths at home with their so-called loved ones. I always found it so irksome, growing up, whenever my mother would be verbally chastising my siblings and me and the phone would ring; and she would pick up the receiver to greet the one on the other end with the sweetest voice and tone.

You have to set the atmosphere by how *you* talk to get your husband to talk to you. When you learn the secret of treating your husband with great respect and honor, he will open up his heart to you because he trusts you with his vulnerable parts.

It's about trust. Men only express their deep feelings and thoughts with whom they trust. If he senses, based on your past behavior, or someone else's in his past, that he is not respected, he will be as closed as an unopened clam.[22]

In the afore mentioned book by David Clarke, a reference is made to what he calls the "Male Zone". This is the place men sometimes go to when their wives are talking to them. It's a place where men tend to zone out and are no longer listening – with absolutely nothing on their minds."[23] He assures us that they don't do it deliberately. As women, we don't understand that, so we badger our husbands to tell us what their thinking about. "Nothing" is not an acceptable answer, so we harass them thinking that will get them to open up. The truth is that it has the opposite effect. All it does is cause our husbands to obstinately refuse to communicate. Clarke says this, "The male zone is just one minor example of a very important truth. Our brains are different, and so the way we think, the way we talk, and the way we process personal information is different. And these differences block us in conversation."[24]

"Model" Behavior

It's very important that we model respectful behavior to our children. We are whom they will use as examples for how to treat their fathers, but it will also teach our daughters how to be in their own homes. This makes me think of the verse, Proverb 13:22a, that tells us, "*Good people leave an inheritance to their grand-children...*" (NLT). The truth is there are all kinds of inheritances besides monetary riches. Children inherit their parent's genes, some personality traits, bad habits, good habits, etc. When this verse talks about leaving an inheritance for one's grandchildren, it simply means that what you are passing along is so strong and lasting that it not only transfers to your children but also your grandchildren.

We are responsible for what we leave behind by way of heritage and legacy. We must weigh everything we do in consideration of how it will affect our children, our children's children and every other seed that follows.

Are you leaving an inheritance? Yes, you are. However, the quality of the type you are leaving is up to you. Let me encourage you to pay attention to what you are doing, saying, and living in front of your children. They are! Will it be something worth carrying into the future?

Let these Scriptures help strengthen your resolve: *If anyone thinks himself to be religious [scrupulously observant of the rituals of his faith], and does not control his tongue but deludes his own heart, this person's religion is worthless (futile, barren)* (James 1:26 AMP); *Let your speech be gracious, seasoned with salt, so that you may know how you should answer every person* (Col. 4:6 CSB).

Once you've made the decision to get your mouth in line with God's Word, you will have to be committed to it even when it doesn't look like it's working. When you change the way you talk, the whole atmosphere of your home will change. It will become a place of refuge, a home where healing takes place – a place where loved ones will run for safety and shelter.

Another way to model respect to your children is by paying attention to your husband when he speaks to you. During one of the times I was working on this book, we had a couple of repair persons in our garage working on our soft-water system. My husband had done research on the system as he was hoping to repair it himself. Although he wasn't successful in his attempt, he still had the instructional manuals handy and was full of ideas and chatter that he wanted to share with me regarding the whole thing. He didn't seem to notice that I was busy, so I stopped what I was doing (at the cost of losing my concentration), to give him my full attention. Initially, I was a tad bit annoyed, but the Holy Spirit reminded me that I was writing about respect and this was one way to exhibit that. I know some of you are probably thinking, "Why wasn't he more sensitive to what was going with you?" I know, and I had to push that thought out of my head in order to obey the Holy Spirit. You see, when it comes to pleasing God, it sometimes means putting aside *our* needs to meet the needs of someone else. As it turned out, I was able to pick right up where I left off without a hitch. Believe it or not, after a bit, he did realize that he was keeping me from something and apologized for interrupting me. God is faithful!

Reflection

WHERE DO YOU GO FROM HERE?

1. How has this section impacted you?

2. How can you apply the things you learned in this section?

3. What can you ask God to help you with?

CHAPTER 5

You're More Powerful Than You Know

S ome very open and vulnerable men have stated how much they need us women. Here are a few notable quotes:

"In that single moment when you glance in our direction, we lock eyes, and all we feel is our heart beating through our chest, you *have* us. And there is absolutely nothing we can do about it!" *-Alexander T. MacGregor, Jr., Editor-in-Chief of The Boulevardier*

"...sometimes we wonder why someone as amazing as you wants to be with us." *-Lalo Fuentes, Celebrity Trainer*

"I wish women understood that no matter how much they may think

their man is evolved, we are very basic. Even the most manscaped guy in a Brooks Brothers suit is a caveman at heart. Let us grunt and be ourselves and we will gladly drag your dinner home."
-Tim Wilkins, Comedian

"One of the truest facts in life is that every man needs a woman when his life is a mess because just like in a game of chess, the queen protects the king. Loyalty and compassion are both traits that many women share, and when a women is in love, she will do whatever is necessary to protect her man and look after his bests interests…and this is why there is a great woman behind every great man." *- Unknown*

A Lesson from, *Nicholas Nickleby*

It's unfortunate, but if we aren't especially vigilant, it is very easy for us to take advantage of our men, and try to take on the leadership role in our homes. Really, it boils down to the fact that when we refuse to respect our husbands, we are essentially saying that we don't believe in their leadership and would rather be the ones in control. Marriage is not meant to be a dictatorship – from either side. It's to be a partnership with equal rights

The novel, *The Life and Adventures of Nicholas Nickleby* by Charles Dickens contains a strikingly brutal excerpt that clearly illustrates the fact that there are actually women in this world who feel it is their mission and duty in life to humiliate men.

It's the story a young man who must support his mother and sister after his father dies. Nicholas, his mother and his younger sister are forced to give up their comfortable lifestyle in Devonshire and travel to London to seek the aid of their only relative, Nicholas's uncle, Ralph Nickleby. Ralph, has no desire to help his destitute relations and hates Nicholas on sight. He gets Nicholas a very low-paying job as an assistant to Wackford Squeers, who runs a school. Squeers and his monstrous wife whip and beat the children regularly, while spoiling their own son. Nicholas is aware of this mistreatment and disapproves.[25]

The following exchange between Mr. and Mrs. Squeers perfectly exemplifies my above point:

> 'He's a nasty stuck-up monkey, that's what I consider him,' said Mrs. Squeers, reverting to Nicholas.

Supposing he is,' said Squeers, 'he is as well stuck up in our schoolroom as anywhere else, isn't he?--especially as he don't like it.'

'Well,' observed Mrs. Squeers, 'there's something in that. I hope it'll bring his pride down, and it shall be no fault of mine if it don't.'

'If you dislike him, my dear,' returned Squeers, 'I don't know anybody who can show dislike better than you, and of course there's no occasion, with him, to take the trouble to hide it.'

'I don't intend to, I assure you,' interposed Mrs. S.

'That's right,' said Squeers; 'and if he has a touch of pride about him, as I think he has, I don't believe there's woman in all England that can bring anybody's spirit down, as quick as you can, my love.'

Mrs. Squeers chuckled vastly on the receipt of these flattering compliments, and said, she hoped she had tamed a high spirit or two in her day. It is but due to her character to say, that in conjunction with her estimable husband, she had broken many and many a one.[26]

I Get It, But...

I totally get it! I fully understand why feminists have taken the stand they have. For far too long, we have had a male-dominated society *-dominated* being the operative word. Unfortunately, it went way beyond just male leadership to the abuse of women by way of sexual harassment and abuse, requiring submission despite verbal and physical abuse, menial pay for the same jobs as men just to name a few. I get it. However, if we call ourselves Christians, then we have a different standard from that of the world. In his commentary on 1 Peter, Dr. Tony Evans says, "Non-Christians should be viewing you as a little strange because you're seeking to conform to God's standards and not to the world's."[27] It's too easy to just stand by and allow a society that is not God-driven to lull us to sleep and accept what they toss our way. When you hear a lie long enough, it starts to sound like the truth. Our standard is the standard of absolute truth that is based on God's Word. Ephesians 5:22b clearly states that wives are to respect their husbands. That does not dismiss the fact that husbands are to cherish and nourish their wives and love them the way Christ loves the Church.

What do you notice when you watch most sitcoms? They portray the husband as an idiot who can do nothing right; and without the help of their wives, they'd be useless. They promote the great intellect and cleverness of the wife to the exclusion of her husband. This depiction saddens me because it is so obviously promoting the agenda of Satan which is, amongst a host of other schemes, to destroy God's idea of the family where the husband is the head, leading his family in righteousness.

Ladies, we must take a position of strength and declare to the world that we will not follow their methods. It may feel like you are standing alone, but if we band together and say, "Not in my house!", we can make a difference. Just imagine the kind of confidence that will rise up in your husband! And trust me when I tell you, when he feels good about himself based on how you treat him, he will treat you like the queen you are. A respectful, honoring wife inspires her husband's loyalty and devotion.

Adrian, my husband, and I were listening to some oldies one weekend. Of course, listening to all those old Motown songs brings back old memories and feelings; but as I paid closer attention to some of the words, a couple of things caught my attention. Many of the artists from that era of music sang about their devotion to the woman in their life. For instance, some of the lyrics in the song, "I'm Your Puppet" sung by James and Bobby Purify, are:

"I'm yours to have and to hold,
Darling you've got full control of your puppet"
"Treat me good, and I'll do anything.
I'm just a puppet and you hold the string"[28]

Here's a man saying, "You treat me well, loving me and honoring me, and you have my heart. I'll do anything for you.

The song, "Ain't No Woman Like the One I've Got" by the Four Tops is another one I felt had such profound lyrics with something in it that one could easily miss if not paying close attention:

"She can build me up when it's down I'm going
Put a little music in my day
Wouldn't be surprised if our love keeps growing
Bigger every minute that she stays away.
I would kiss the ground she walks on
'Cause it's my word, my word she'll obey now,
hoo hoo."[29]

That just wouldn't be complete without the "hoo hoo". In this particular song, I imagine that, perhaps, someone listening with a negatively-critical ear would pounce on the phrase in the song that announces, "Cause it's my word she'll obey…" What independent, free-thinking, modern woman would dare *obey* some man! The one saying that has completely missed the line before that declared, "I would kiss the ground she walks on." In my opinion, this describes a man fully devoted to an honoring and respectful woman – not just in love with, but fully devoted to. Devotion is defined as **ardent, often selfless affection and dedication,** as to **a person or principle.**[30] Who wouldn't want that experience.

Reflection

WHERE DO YOU GO FROM HERE?

1. How has this section impacted you?

2. How can you apply the things you learned in this section?

3. What can you ask God to help you with?

CHAPTER 6

The Accomplished Woman's Playbook

n the world we live in now, it isn't difficult at all to find a great woman leader. We're all over the place in every arena of life. When you look at science, technology, engineering, arts and mathematics even government, we have definitely come a long way (with still a long way to go), and our accomplishments cannot be ignored.

That's the good news. The bad news, however, is that all those accomplishments, sometimes, come with great sacrifices. If not being exceptionally alert, we women could be guilty of putting success in our careers above the needs of our families. Jackie Kennedy Onassis once said (One of my favorite quotes, by the way), "If you bungle raising your children, I don't think whatever else you do matters very much." I wholeheartedly agree with her assessment. However, I would add that if you bungle nurturing your *relationship* with children or husband despite all you may accomplish and all the accolades you receive, whatever else you do matters very little.

As women, accomplished or otherwise, we have this God-given "inwardness" to nurture. We will always nurture someone or something; and if we don't have our priorities well established, we will nurture everyone else but those nearest us.

Most women find it unconscionable to neglect their children, so they are less likely to do so. On the other hand, it's a little easier to neglect our husbands. Why? Because we expect them to be mature and understanding – that they are old enough to fend for themselves. Surely they understand when we have other obligations that keep us busy and occupied, like a business call at home that keeps us tied up for hours. But this is where it gets tricky. If you haven't already established and laid the groundwork first, he will *no*t be understanding or mature and may, in fact, resent your success and thus, resent you.

There is this delicate and, sometimes, awkward dance that husbands and wives do especially when the wife is a in a strong leadership role in her career, perhaps in a high-level managerial or executive position. Being able to allow herself to take on a more submissive role in the home can be a bit troublesome for her. However, where we are leaders in some instances, it's necessary to be a follower in other occasions. Your home is one of those instances.

Demonstrating respect to your husband can be found in simply and biblically submitting to your husband's leadership. I'm not talking about you living under a dictatorship or that your husband is the "big boss" and you're the lowly employee or servant. The role of followers is to help leaders be more effective while remaining true to their own values and essential needs.

You can be a follower and still be a leader even in your home. Peter F. Drucker, prolific management writer, said, "Leadership is lifting a person's vision to higher sights, the raising of a person's performance to a higher standard, the building of a personality beyond its normal limitations." Isn't that what we want for our husbands? Allowing them the respect and honor they so crave will help them soar to heights they never dreamed possible. You can create a giant of a husband or a dwarf simply by the words you speak to him and about him. Allowing him to lead the way God intended will go a very long way in creating an atmosphere where you both can grow and flourish.

Sometimes it's easy to become disrespectful when

you find yourself competing with your husband for authority in the home. We need to stay in our lanes and not try to take over just because we have the skill to do so. Remember, you are not competitors but partners. You each have gifts that, combined, make an unstoppable force. However, you will never get to experience that "force" if you are vying for the upper hand.

Forgiveness plays a pretty big role in being able to deliver respect to your husband on a consistent basis. You husband is bound to do something that agitates or annoys you. He is certain to offend you in some way or other. Unfortunately, that does not give us permission to decide that he does not deserve our respect. On the contrary, it's under those circumstances that we have to work the hardest at it. It's all too easy to forget why we do the things we do. Remember, it's God we are ultimately trying to please, not necessarily our mate. When we make pleasing God our goal, it will naturally spill over and bless our mates.

Reflection

WHERE DO YOU GO FROM HERE?

1. How has this section impacted you?

2. How can you apply the things you learned in this section?

3. What can you ask God to help you with?

TYING IT ALL TOGETHER:

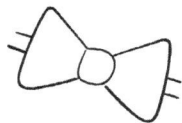

Some Final Words

A woman who knows how to compose a soup or a salad that is perfectly harmonious in flavour ought to be clever at mixing together the sweet and harsh elements of a man's character, and she will understand how to charm and keep forever her husband's heart and soul."[30]

Let me encourage you to not grow weary in doing well (Galatians 6:9). This is where trust in our Heavenly Father comes into play. It's easy to wish that your husband would learn all the particular needs that you have as you are learning his, but that Scripture also goes on tell us that we'll reap at the proper time if we don't give up. So, hang in there and be steadfast and immovable in your decision to do things God's way. You are not forgotten; God sees you.

I recognize that I may have taken too simplistic an approach for some in understanding the needs of men, but the truth is, unless you want to do a full psychological and physiological study of men, simplicity is the best approach, in my opinion.

So, Well Fed, Well Sexed, Well Respected! If you desire to recharge your married life, taking these three simple, but oh so profound, understandings to heart will launch it into another realm. Now, if I can just convince my husband to write a book for men regarding us women. It will probably have to be much longer because, as I stated in the outset, **WOMEN ARE SO MUCH MORE COMPLICATED!**

End Notes

1. Richard Tolivar, *Woman, A Godly Creation* (Arizona: Saguaro Publishing Co., 2014) p.2.
2. Danielle Paquette, Washington Post West African Bureau Chief. "Why Men and Women Treat Food Differently", Sept. 15, 2015.
3. Ibid.
4. Ibid.
5. Amanda McMillan, "Surprising ways Men and Women Sense Things Differently", 2015 Health Magazine (health.com).
6. Walter Trobisch, *I Loved a Girl*, (New York: Harper and Row 1965) p. 3.
7. Dr. Juli Slattterly, *No More Headaches, Enjoying Sex and Intimacy in Marriage* (Illinois: Tyndale House Publishers 2009) , Kindle location1413.
8. Ibid, Kindle location 1433.
9. Ibid, Kindle location 1444.

10. Ibid, Kindle location 1517.

11. Lexico..com, Oxford English and Spanish Dictionary.

12. Rape in America: A Report to the Nation, Arlington, VA , April 29, 1992.

13. Tim and Beverly LaHaye, *The Act of Marriage*, pages (Michigan: Zondervan 1976) p.45-47.

14. Lester Sumrall, *60 Things God Said About Sex*©-Lester Sumrall, 1993, (Indiana:LaSEA Publishing Co.) p.8.

15. John Bolte, *"How Much Sex Should Couples be Having?"*, Feb. 7 2020 ©USA Today, a Division of Gannet Satelite Information.

16. Ibid.

17. Mary Andres, co-director of the Master's Program and professor of Clinical Education at University of Southern California.

18. Howard J Clinebell and Charlotte H. Clinebell, The Intimate Marriage, p. 29. (New York: Harper and Row,1970) p.29.

19. Lester Sumrall *60 Things God Said About Sex*, ©Lester Sumrall, 1993, (Indiana:LaSEA Publishing Co.) p.57.

20. Jerry Bock, *Fiddler on the Roof* (from the Broadway musical. [United States]: RCA Victor, 1964.

21. David Clark, PhD, *Men are Clams, Women are Crowbars.* (Ohio: Promised Press, 1998).

22. Ibid pp. 11-17.

23. Ibid p. 87.

24. Ibid p.87.

25. Wikipedia Contributors: Nicholas Nickleby, Wikipedia, the Free Encyclopedia, 8 December 2020. Web. December 2020.

26. Charles Dickens, *The Life and Adventures of Nicholas Nickleby* (DB Publishing House 2011) pp. 88-89.

27. Tony Evans, *The Tony Evans Bible Commentary.* (Holman Bible Publishers, 2019, Nashville, TN, p.1353.

28. Dan Penn and Spencer Oldham, "I'm Your Puppet" (Papa Don Enterprises, 1965).

29. Dennis Lambert and Brian Potter, "Ain't No Woman Like the One I've Got" (ABC/Dunhill Records, 1972).

30. Kennerman English Multilingual Dictionary (K Dictionaries, Ltd, 2006-2013.

31. Berjane, "French Dishes for English Tables" (MFK Fisher's Translation of the Physiology of Taste, 1931).

About the Author

PAMELA A. STOVALL,
Well Fed, Well Sexed, Well Respected!

Life and marriage coach, communication expert, and conference speaker Pamela, has seen a lot and heard a lot by talking with women from all walks of life. She states, frequently, "The experiences some of the women I endeavor to help in their marriages and life, in general, would curl your hair if it's straight or straighten if it's curly!"

A former educator and mother of three, Pamela lives happily with her husband of many, many years in the

Greater Phoenix Metro Area. She has co-authored the book *Marriage is Not for the Faint of Heart* with him, as well as authored and compiled *Just So You Know: Spicy Wisdom for Young Christian Women*. She even has a children's book, *Charlotte and the Yellow Dress*, added to her resumé.

Pamela is available for speaking opportunities. You may reach her at sacredcovenantministries@yahoo.com. You might also check out her and her husband's website: sacredcovenantministries.com where they write a weekly blog.

www.ingramcontent.com/pod-product-compliance
Lightning Source LLC
Chambersburg PA
CBHW062144020426
42334CB00020B/2505